THE LAST MASTODON

D0778313

Christina Olson

Rattle | *Studio City, California* | 2019

The Last Mastodon
Copyright © 2019 by Christina Olson

Layout and design by Timothy Green

Cover image by Christina Olson

ISBN: 978-1-931307-43-7

First edition

Rattle Foundation
12411 Ventura Blvd
Studio City, CA 91604
www.rattle.com

Contents

THE LAST MASTODON

AUTHOR'S NOTE

In summer of 2017, I was invited to serve as poet-in-residence for a paleontology conference and exhibition ("The Valley of the Mastodons") at the Western Science Center in Hemet, California.

These pieces were inspired by that time spent among the paleontologists as well as my observations of the museum's collections of fossils, particularly Max the Mastodon.

More information can be found at the end of the chapbook.

Catalogue of Damages

All these years not knowing
the difference between mammoth

and mastodon: just another
human so proud in her indifference.

It's in the teeth: mammoth teeth
resemble the rubber sole of a snow boot—

mastodon teeth, jagged mountains
turned to granite after all these years.

Jefferson thought the West still crawled
with mastodons, sent Lewis & Clark to thin the herd.

All morning I've tried to reconcile
our ambition with the misery it brings:

what we set out to do & what disaster ensues.

Eleven foot at the shoulder, Max
is the largest mastodon in the West.

Jefferson owned Sally Hemings.
I never could make small talk with my father.

I told you this was a catalogue of damages.
Oh god, the mouth is such a weapon.

Origin Story: Max Mastodon

my feet disappear · in prints stamped by mastodons

this morning, I mistook · mountains for shadow
until I shook jetlag, remembered · that in California, magic is possible

the paleontologists know · this already, their days

are long with shadow · their fingernails caked with matrix

and in a lake, bones slumber · and we pull some to shore
a collection of human bones · is a *cemetery*, but these we call a *museum*

bones under our feet · bones washing into the light
some bones · we will call *Max*

Who Gets to Be a Fossil

Max the mastodon gets to be a fossil.

Thomas Jefferson gets to be a fossil.

Max lived 14,000 years ago in a scrub forest filled with lizards & quail.

Thomas Jefferson built Monticello & signed the Declaration of Independence.

Sometimes Max used his tusks to fight other mastodons & sometimes his tusk would pierce the skull of other male he was fighting & that mastodon died.

I Google *Where is Thomas Jefferson buried* & the answer is on a website run by a woman named Carol who posts pictures of the graves of Thomas Jefferson & his family.

Carol writes, *Something of a disappointment was the fact that the locked wrought iron fence prohibited visitors from paying homage to the great man & his family.*

Max kept wandering through the California scrub until he died & his bones turned hard & then some men in hats found them when they were digging a dam.

Carol's website also features a recipe for Carol's Low Fat Peanut Soup & something called Crock Pot Dinner of Beans, Kale & Sausage for Three.

Jefferson fathered six children with his slave Sally Hemings. Four lived to adulthood, which means Sally would need to make Dinner of Beans & Kale times one & one-third to feed their children.

The mastodons are dead & you & I will never see them.

[...]

Carol writes, *Somehow it felt as if we were being banned from his world.*

Sally Hemings may have lived in a room in Monticello's South Dependencies, a wing of the mansion accessible to the main house through a covered passageway.

Carol writes, *Thomas Jefferson belongs to his United States of America for time eternal.*

Sally Hemings belonged to Thomas Jefferson for time eternal, or until he died.

Max the mastodon belongs to the Western Science Center in Hemet, California & people pay to look at him because he is a very impressive mastodon fossil, the biggest found west of the Mississippi River.

Thomas Jefferson is buried at Monticello, behind a wrought iron fence that prevents unwanted visitors.

Sally Hemings was buried in a site in downtown Charlottesville, Virginia, which is now covered by the parking lot of the Hampton Inn on West Main Street.

Wake Up, Little Stevie

Little Stevie, a mastodon who lived 50,000 years ago,
is interred at the Western Science Center

in another dimension the mastodons are still alive
their teeth not yet white marble hard as a Venus's breast
and in another dimension the ocean has not yet receded like a hairline
and the freeway does not yet hold California together like sutures
and the water in Diamond Valley Lake sparkles like nothing
because there is not water, there is no lake and the mastodons
are not hardening in their muddy graves they are instead pissing
and fighting and breathing like you did this morning
and in another dimension the great tusks are not slumbering in the tar,
waiting to be dragged out of the black rot
and in another dimension you are Little Stevie lumbering in the scrub
and you are not thinking about death but rather dinner
and in another dimension you are alive, you are alive, not dead, no, never dead

How to Care for Your American Mastodon

Mammut pacificus

Experience: Advanced. *Size*: 13 feet at the shoulder. *Lifespan*: Dead. *Habitat*: Gone. Or, rather, here, but different now. *Care*: Your mastodon requires wide expanses to graze and forage. An adult mastodon consumes nearly three pounds of coniferous twigs a day. They prefer the tender greens. Brittle twigs will stick in a mastodon's throat. Your baby mastodon will spend most of its early life huddled against its mother in the cold spruce woodlands. Like you, it will learn to navigate. Or it will die. Hang a heat bulb over the dry side of the habitat. Decorate with scrub and quail. Always lift at the midsection, not by the legs. Always wash your hands before (and after) handling your mastodon. Let your mastodon settle into its new surroundings for the first three or four days after you bring it home. If you see any of these symptoms, take your mastodon to the vet for a check-up: hiding most of the time; minimal eating or drinking; drinking too much; discharge from eyes, nose, or mouth; mastodon is dead; mastodon is just bones. If you have more questions about your mastodon's health, talk to a veterinarian familiar with mastodons. If you find one, let us know.

Self-Portrait as Mastodon Remains

the skull has been punched once   twice

     eleven thousand years later, the paleontologist

fits another tusk into the holes & sees

     what damage the mouth can wreak

once upon an epoch, one mastodon bleeds out

     & another one has a killer toothache

mastodon, no one ever told you that a hairy coat

     hides all the blood   or that the head

weeps from any hole it sees fit to

     when your bones are resettled in the flood

do not mourn the scattering of jaw from rib

     & hasn't the heart begged free from the tongue

when they find what remains of your mouth, smile

     finally revealed despite the blue effort of glacier

mastodon: the words *breast* + *tooth* in Greek

     that was my last kiss   my best kiss

Animals Doing Things to Other Animals

In the Page Museum at La Brea Tar Pits in California, the skulls of wolves glow orange. Their sheer number is difficult to comprehend.

The most populous specimen found at La Brea is not mastodon, but dire wolf. 4000 skulls and fragments, pulled free from tar.

Jefferson owned more than 600 slaves during his lifetime. He freed ten.

℘ ෬

Bones from a tar pit are stained brown.

℘ ෬

Two of the freed were the children Jefferson had with Sally Hemings. Hemings negotiated this in exchange for returning to Virginia from France. She was sixteen.

Madison and Eston were freed upon Jefferson's death. Beverly and Harriet disappeared. Or rather, they passed.

℘ ෬

The scientists at the pit work 361 days a year.

At Monticello, six hundred men, women, children worked 365 days a year.

℘ ෬

La Brea means *the tar*, so to say *the La Brea tar pits* is to say *the the tar tar pits*. It is a stutter, a tripped tongue.

Sometimes visitors to La Brea mistake the scientists for actors, or for robots. A certain type of tourist mistakes industry for theatre.

Stutter: involuntary sound repetition, but also hesitation or pausing.

℘ ℭ

I meant they passed as white.

℘ ℭ

To say *black people were enslaved* is redundancy. Of course they were black. Mulatto. Quadroon. One drop is all it takes.

℘ ℭ

The brain cannot comprehend some things, and thus we stutter.

℘ ℭ

Sally Hemings was Martha Jefferson's half-sister. Jefferson never remarried after Martha's death at age thirty-three.

In one version of the truth, Jefferson did not remarry because he loved Martha and honored her deathbed promise.

But this is also true: Jefferson did not need to remarry. He had Sally.

℘ ℭ

[...]

A stutter hangs awkwardly, the sounds sticking in the mouth.

Jefferson, of course, is thought to have stuttered.

℘ ℛ

The fields surrounding Monticello are green and brown and black. In the winter, they sometimes freeze.

At La Brea, it smells of asphalt. A thick bubble inflates, then pops.

I wish I could call my father, tell him where I stand.

℘ ℛ

I watch a boy, captivated by the bubble. He is standing next to a life-size model of a ground sloth. Around him are the bones of condors, saber-toothed tigers, an army of wolves. But they are dead, and thus hard to understand. They are a concept.

The bubble is real. He sees himself in its darkness.

℘ ℛ

What do we do now, my country. The situation grows dire.

℘ ℛ

A tar pit is a black trap. But it also supports life: bacteria, extremophiles.

Under the harshest conditions, something endures.

How to Care for Your Yesterday's Camel

Camelops hesternus

Let your *Camelops* drink too much when it is sad. Let it slump with the short-faced bear on a vinyl stool, bitch about lazy nomenclature. All the words in the world, and *Camelops* got *camel face*. Let it order whiskey, let it get, yes, camelfaced. So much we don't know. And even paleontologists work in spit and prayer. When only bones remain, reconstruction errors abound. A gentle hump of fat might soften a profile, ease a jaw. But millennia pass, adipose melts. One day, even humans will be reassembled wrong. If we are lucky, they will make us taller, kinder than we ever were.

Among the Bones

Another year without my father,
another year spent bringing

home bones from the woods.
On my desk are dead things:

a jar of the dog's white fur
that the vet shaved to better

see the last needle in.
A porcupine skull rippled

with sutures. Oyster halves.
I spilled a glass of wine

on the sand dollar, but the next
morning, head throbbing,

I bleached it back to normal.
That first day shadowing

the paleontologist, I was afraid
to touch the ridged tooth

of mammoth. I used two
fingers, like I would a baby

whose skull hasn't set.
You're not going to hurt it,

said the paleontologist.
She was measuring a tusk.

It survived fifteen thousand years
in the ground. Among the bones

in that cool room, I felt
the weight of something

like geology. Drawers
and cabinets filled with pieces

of dead things. The jumble
of bison teeth. Ancient

horses so plentiful, no one
bothers to catalog them.

After the vet left the house,
I plucked the puff of fur

from the trash, put it in a jar.
The advantage to dead things

is that you cannot hurt them
anymore. Instead, they hurt you,

over and over and over.
The fur in its jar, the skull

of a northern mockingbird—
the impossible lightness of grief.

Reconstruction Errors, Part 1 & 2

1.

All day I've tried & failed to write
this letter to you. Do we deserve anything
for our failings, our clumsy fumblings
in the dark? I have no excuse
for this dizziness, the sober way
I lurch from truth to truth.
The sky can't decide between bruise
or blue; in this way, it is like the heart.
We were a long time ago, you & I—
we had all our original teeth. You sent
me a video of the lake, the rustle
of blue on the rocks. I weep because our dog
is dying, because I haven't smelled
fresh water for such a long time.
That summer, I visited La Brea twice.
It gave my pain some geological perspective.
The surface of the tar pit shone
blue-black, reflected the sky, smelled
of street. But I forgot my science:
there are more predators than prey
in the pits, the bones dragged to the light.

2.

But I forgot my science: there are more predators
than prey in the pits, the bones dragged to the light—
original teeth. The surface of the tar pit
shone blue-black, reflected the smell of street.

You sent me a video of the lake, the rustle of blue
on the rocks. Do we deserve anything for our fumblings,
these clumsy failings in the dark? The sky can't decide
between bruise or blue; in this way, it is like the heart.
I have no excuse for this dizziness, the sober way
I lurch from truth to truth. We were a long time ago,

you & I. That summer, I visited La Brea twice.
It gave my pain some geological perspective. I weep
because our dog is dying, because I haven't smelled water
for such a long time. All day I've tried & failed.

Self-Portrait as Mammoth Remains

The remains of Xena, a 12-foot high
Mammuthus columbi, *is on display*
at the Western Science Center

Xena, forgive me but you're just not that interesting

Xena, did they name you for that dumb t.v. show

Xena, you could have lived to eighty but you quit at twenty

Xena, you weren't even woolly

Xena, your left tusk is blunter than your right, which made you a lefty

Xena, *sinister* in Latin means *left* & *unlucky* but *right* in English means *proper*

Xena, you're probably a male after all

Xena, that's not a joke, we've been looking at your tusks & we have a hypothesis

Xena, Max is nearly as tall as you are & he's just a mastodon

Xena, your species' namesake is Columbus, who wasn't all that great

Xena, what is it with these early paleontologists & their goddamn heroes

Xena, what is it with all these goddamned flawed men

Xena, now you're one of them

Xena, did you even stand a chance

Xena, did you like it deep underground where you lay before they dug out the lake

Xena, was everyone finally quiet

Xena, did you learn to still your mind

and will you teach me how

Broken Sonnet on Teeth

Smilodo fatalis

I told you about the mammoth tooth, flat
and waffled like snow boots—and its cousin
the mastodon, its molars like *breasts*, that sin—
but at La Brea everyone wants to see the cat,
Smilodon, eight-inch knives in its mouth that
even now haunt our dreams—we are running,
we are losing the race, then, behind us, a pant in
the ear, single hot breath and we are down, flat—
that's the end of that human's story. We fear the knife
of the sabre-tooth, its name a clear warning, but we
miss its point—*Smilodon* died when its big prey
died out, but we'll expire when the smallest life
on Earth does. Surely you've noticed the bees
have gone quiet? Forget teeth. Time to pray.

I Am a Giant Ground Sloth,
I Am Not a Giant Ground Sloth

clumsy, slow-moving // difficulty regulating its body temperature // & haven't you sweat more this summer than you have in years // a constellation of fat around your belly // the dark hair sprouting from chin

the *Megalonyx* lives in families, but *Paramylodon* is a loner // Harlan's ground sloth never lived in the desert or the upper Midwest // & didn't your seven years there nearly kill you

& even when you wanted to stay, the prairie pushed you away // all that soy // all that sky

Paramylodon dragged itself across the ground // never climbed a tree // never wanted to be closer to the sky

some days you are half-sloth // half-armadillo // but at night you dream of cats

they found fossil sloth tracks pressed into prison grounds in Nevada // the prison since closed but at night the license plates & sloths crawl again

under the skin of the ground sloth are dermal ossicles // chips of bone under the skin // the body is just a bag of rocks & skin // we carry our stones with us in our shoulders

[...]

in your right heel is a shard of glass // & some weeks you feel it working
its way closer to the surface // like old bone // like old pain

Jefferson thought the sloth claw sent from Lewis & Clark was an extant
lion // and on some days doesn't your own reflection catch you by surprise
// that new mane

The Last Mastodon

Every time I type *tusk* on my phone, it autocorrects to *risk*.

The French for *tusks* is *défenses*.

෫ ଷ

Max, I call you the last mastodon. You weren't, of course.

෫ ଷ

I have been collecting reconstruction errors—the early, wrong assemblies. The first mastodons on display had the tusks facing the wrong way, like digging tools. A giant rodent who tunneled underground.

The Niederweningen mammoth had its tusks pointed outward, like the enormous mustaches fashionable at the time.

In yet another early drawing, a mastodon is trunkless, earless, looks like a boar with killer teeth splayed.

Our imaginations run wild, fail us. We are constantly revising.

෫ ଷ

Jefferson hoped that the mastodon still lived in the West so that he could prove the French wrong. It was a pissing contest. Which country was younger, stronger, superior? Which country had unexplored acres where mastodons towered over men? He died refusing to believe that his mastodon could be extinct. Sally was down the hall.

[...]

When it comes to death, we are all magical thinkers.

$\wp \; \text{Q}\!\!\!\text{R}$

The scientists know what I do not: their work will never be finished.

I am not a scientist, and so I keep thinking something will click into place, something will indicate completion.

$\wp \; \text{Q}\!\!\!\text{R}$

One night, we were driven high into the mountains above the lake, where the desert gives way to pine. We drank whiskey at the bar, and on the way back down, we sang "The River" and "O Canada" and we pulled off in a grapefruit grove to piss and pluck fruit.

This is not a story about mastodons. This is a story about humans, our animal ways.

$\wp \; \text{Q}\!\!\!\text{R}$

Here is a story making the rounds at the conference: somewhere in Virginia, a man in his 80s has a mastodon tusk as a household object, and his wife decorates it for each season. Some months the tusk is topped with a Santa hat; some months, it wears rabbit ears.

This story bothers me, and then I remember my desk at home: the skull of the porcupine, the fur we pulled from the dog as he died, the oyster shells never returned to the sea.

What is it about humans, why do we love to collect the dead.

$\wp \; \text{Q}\!\!\!\text{R}$

Here is another story someone tells me: in Costa Rica, he observed three-toed sloths eating human waste from the latrine. He says that we are all opportunistic.

Then he pauses, says, *Except for koalas.*

෨ ଔ

I apologize for only thinking about bones these last few months. But maybe I should apologize for not thinking of them sooner.

෨ ଔ

From the paleontologists, I learn to ask: *What does this mean?*

෨ ଔ

My father was a geologist, not a paleontologist. Still, he collected things to display: a trilobite in dark matrix, a fossil of a fish. I once asked him if I could bring the fish to school for show and tell, and he agreed. He showed me how to wrap it in a dish towel for safekeeping, and then we tucked it carefully into a burgundy Tupperware.

At school, no one cared about the fish fossil. The teacher tried to make it interesting, but I knew that the other kids were bored. Who cares about dead things?

I'm surprised he ever let me take the fossil, watched me climb the elementary school steps with the Tupperware in both hands.

How easily everything can be broken. How strong some things must be to endure.

෨ ଔ

[...]

And somewhere in Siberia, the men are at work bringing back Max's relative, the woolly mammoth. They want the new mammoth to roam the tundra by 2039—a year that looks preposterous. A typo.

This is what men do: they tear things apart, then put them back together.

℘ ℭ

As one paleontologist told me on the last day: *Maybe. Maybe not.*

℘ ℭ

At the Western Science Center, the displayed fossils are set on cork. In case of earthquake, they are designed to drop back into the ground for safekeeping.

When California crumbles, Max will go back to his earth.

A Story About Bones

as it turns out, paleontology & poetry

    are not all that different

both the excavating of a shard

    here & there, an attempt to see what fits

the painstaking assembly of meaning from fragments

    maybe if you get lucky: a tooth, pointed—

the people in their practical clothes & boots

    sometimes even the same tiny brushes

& at the museum I kept calling the collections *stacks*

    but instead of *poem* let's just say *word cage*

all morning I've been laboring at this—

    the way I regard something for hours, come back

& in the new light over the desk, something's shifted

    suddenly I see the tusk, the femur

or the weapon, how it fits in my hand

    like it's always been there   like I never put it down

ACKNOWLEDGMENTS

The poem "Self-Portrait as Mastodon Remains" first appeared in *Alaska Quarterly Review* and was subsequently reprinted on *Poetry Daily*.

The poem "Catalogue of Damages" was selected by *Broadsided Press* and will be released as a broadside in December 2019.

The poems "Reconstruction Errors, Part 1 & 2" and "I Am a Giant Ground Sloth, I Am Not a Giant Ground Sloth" will appear in *Western Humanities Review*.

"Reconstruction Errors, Part 1 & 2" is a poetic form I call the mastodon. More about the form, including its rules, can be found at *Superstition Review*'s blog.

I stole the title framework for "I Am a Giant Ground Sloth, I Am Not a Giant Ground Sloth" from my friend Jean. I'm sorry, Jean.

I am indebted to the Western Science Center and its staff for letting a poet hang out for three days in August 2017. Thank you to the paleontologists and other writers present during that time for their patient answers to my questions. Thank you to Dr. Alton Dooley, Dr. Brett Dooley, and Brittney Stoneburg in particular.

Massive thanks to my friend Dr. Katy Smith, who co-organized "The Valley of the Mastodons" and invited me to Hemet in the first place.

Thanks to my father, Cliff, who hooked me on fossils at an early age.

Learn more about Max, Little Stevie, Xena, and the others at the Western Science Center's website, *westernsciencecenter.org*.

About the Rattle Chapbook Series

The Rattle Chapbook Series publishes and distributes a chapbook to all of *Rattle*'s print subscribers along with each quarterly issue of the magazine. Most selections are made through the annual Rattle Chapbook Prize competition (deadline: January 15th). For more information, and to order other chapbooks from the series, visit our website.

www.Rattle.com/chapbooks